With love for my wingman, Skip Jeffery —S.M.

To Jesse —M.P.

Acknowledgments: The author would like to thank Dr. Robert
E. Gill Jr., project leader—Shorebird Research, United States
Geologic Survey, Alaska Science Center, for sharing his
enthusiasm and expertise. Also a special thank-you to Skip
Jeffery for his support during the creative process.

Millbrook Press
A division of Lerner Publishing Group, Inc.
241 First Avenue North
Minneapolis, MN 55401 USA

For reading levels and more information, look up this title at www.lernerbooks.com.

Main body text set in Sunshine Regular 19/28. Typeface provided by Chank.

Markle, Sandra.
    The long, long journey : the godwit's amazing migration / by Sandra
  Markle ; illustrated by Mia Posada.
      p. cm.
    ISBN 978-0-7613-5623-3 (lib. bdg. : alk. paper)
    ISBN 978-1-4677-1051-0 (eBook)
    1. Bar-tailed godwit—Juvenile literature. 2. Bar-tailed godwit—Migration—
  Juvenile literature. I. Posada, Mia. II. Title.
  QL696.C48M33 2013
  598.3'3—dc23   2012020915

Manufactured in the United States of America
2 – CG – 2/1/14

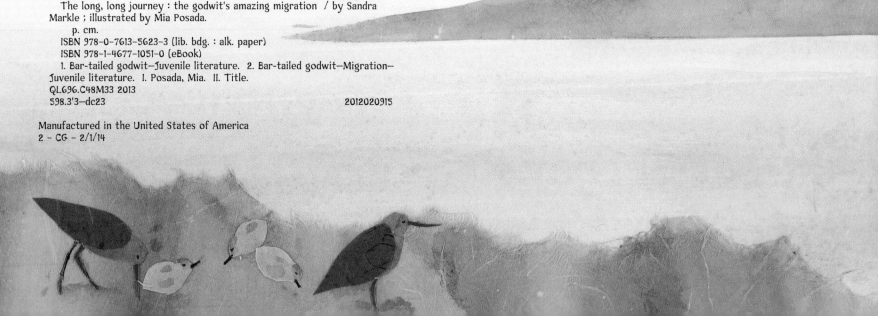

THE LONG, LONG JOURNEY
THE GODWIT'S AMAZING MIGRATION

SANDRA MARKLE
ILLUSTRATIONS BY MIA POSADA

MILLBROOK PRESS • MINNEAPOLIS

Crackle! Crackle! Crunch! The little female bar-tailed godwit at last breaks free of her egg. She steps into the world on long, wobbly legs. It's nearly midnight, but it's June in Alaska and still light. A cool wind blows the chick's downy coat. She shivers, lifts her beak, and squeaks, "Peep! Peep!"

The little female was the last to hatch. Two sisters
and a brother are nearby, with their father. They are
hunting insects in the grass. Their mother next to the
nest trills softly, and the chicks come running.

They huddle with their sister, and their mother settles over them. This way, the newest chick stays warm and joins the family.

For two days, the chicks stay close to the nest. Their parents take turns sitting on them to keep them warm. In between these rests, parents and chicks search for food. The parents need to double their body weight before fall. The chicks need to grow up and become strong.

The little female learns to hunt spiders, crane fly larvae, and beetles. She eats all she can find.

Soon the little godwit and her family wander farther as they feed. But they are rarely alone. Lots of other godwits nest and feed in this treeless land. Sometimes other hunters come searching for food too.

One day, an Arctic fox sneaks up and slips close to the little female.

But her father spots the
fox and squawks a warning.

The little female is not yet able to fly. She crouches low and stays still. Her coloring helps her blend in with the grass. Her father flaps his wings and swoops at the fox.

Her mother joins the attack and so do other adult godwits. The fox runs off without its meal.

For almost a month, the female godwit chick eats and eats and grows bigger. She also grows feathers and loses her fluffy down coat.

When the chick isn't eating,
she's hopping and flapping
her wings. Her wings grow
stronger with each hop-flap.

Then one day, the young female
godwit hops and flaps hard.

For the first time, she does
what godwits do best.

She flies.

In mid-August, the mother godwit leaves. The young birds stay near their father. They eat and practice flying hour after hour so their wings grow even stronger. At last, they follow their father to the coast. They join thousands of godwits gathered on Alaska's Cape Avinof mudflats.

The young female prances across the mud on her long legs. Every step or two, she pokes her long beak deep into the muddy ground to find and eat tunneling worms and tiny clams.

In September, flock after flock of adult
godwits leave the mudflats.

By mid-October, mostly only young birds
remain. The young female is one of the flock.
She practices flying with the other godwits.
In between flights, she feeds alongside them.
She eats and eats, growing very plump.

Finally, when dark clouds sweep
overhead, the young female rises
with the flock. She is pushed
southward by strong winds.
Her long journey has begun.

The young female flies
through unfamiliar skies and
over unknown seas.

Although not one young bird has made this flight before, together they know the route to take. The young female squawks again and again as she flies. By listening for other godwit voices, she stays with the flock even in thick clouds and heavy rain.

One day, a peregrine falcon hunting over an island swoops out of the clouds with wings folded and talon-tipped toes stretched out.

The falcon aims straight for the young female, but she pumps her wings hard, climbs fast, and escapes! Another godwit isn't so lucky.

Day after day and night after night, for nearly eight days, the godwits keep flying.

The young female is thin.
Her wings stroke slower.
Still, she keeps going.

Finally, there's green and brown ahead.

The young female swoops down with
the flock to the New Zealand mudflats,
where land mingles with the sea.

She arrives with two final wing flaps and lands on wobbly legs. Then folding her wings, she falls asleep.

The young female doesn't sleep for long, though. She needs to eat to get back her strength. She'll stay in New Zealand for two years until she's ready to raise a family of her own. Then, when March brings cool winds, she'll once again join the godwit flock and make the long, long journey back to Alaska.

GODWITS ARE AMAZING!

* Godwit chicks hatch after about twenty-one days. They are able to walk, swim, and find their own food almost immediately.

* Godwit adults getting ready to migrate molt and grow new feathers. In spring and summer, their feathers are reddish. By the time godwits begin their migration in September and October, their feathers are gray-brown. When they leave, over half their body weight is fat. This fat gives them the energy they need for the long flight.

* In 2007, researchers fitted one female bar-tailed godwit with a tracking device. Scientists studying the bird discovered that she flew nonstop for 7,270 miles (11,700 kilometers) from Alaska to New Zealand. Godwits don't fly nonstop on the return trip, however. They stop to feed for weeks or even more than a month in the Yellow Sea region of Korea and China. Then, when they arrive in Alaska, they are strong enough to mate and raise a new generation of godwit young.

FIND OUT MORE

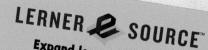

Bar-Tailed Godwit
http://en.wikipedia.org/wiki/File:Bar-tailed_Godwit95.ogg
Play the video to watch a bar-tailed godwit feeding on a mudflat.

Cleary, Brian P. *Sparrow, Eagle, Penguin, and Seagull: What Is a Bird?*
Minneapolis: Millbrook Press, 2013.
This book explains the key characteristics all birds share, playfully introducing this animal group with rhyming verse and comical illustrations.

Elphick, Jonathan. *Atlas of Bird Migration: Tracing the Great Journeys of the World's Birds.* Toronto: Firefly Books, 2007.
You can use this book to compare the bar-tailed godwits' migration to the long-distance journeys of other birds.

The Long Trek of the Bar-Tailed Godwit
http://www.npr.org/templates/story/story.php?storyId=95997182
Listen to biologist Robert Gill tell the story of how his research team discovered the godwits' incredible migration story.

Nelson, Robin. *Migration.* Minneapolis: Lerner Publications Company, 2011.
This book for young readers uses simple text and color photos to show how a number of different animals migrate.

USGS: Bar-Tailed Godwit Photos
http://alaska.usgs.gov/science/biology/shorebirds/barg_photos.html
Investigate this bird's life, and join researchers studying the godwit's marathon flight.

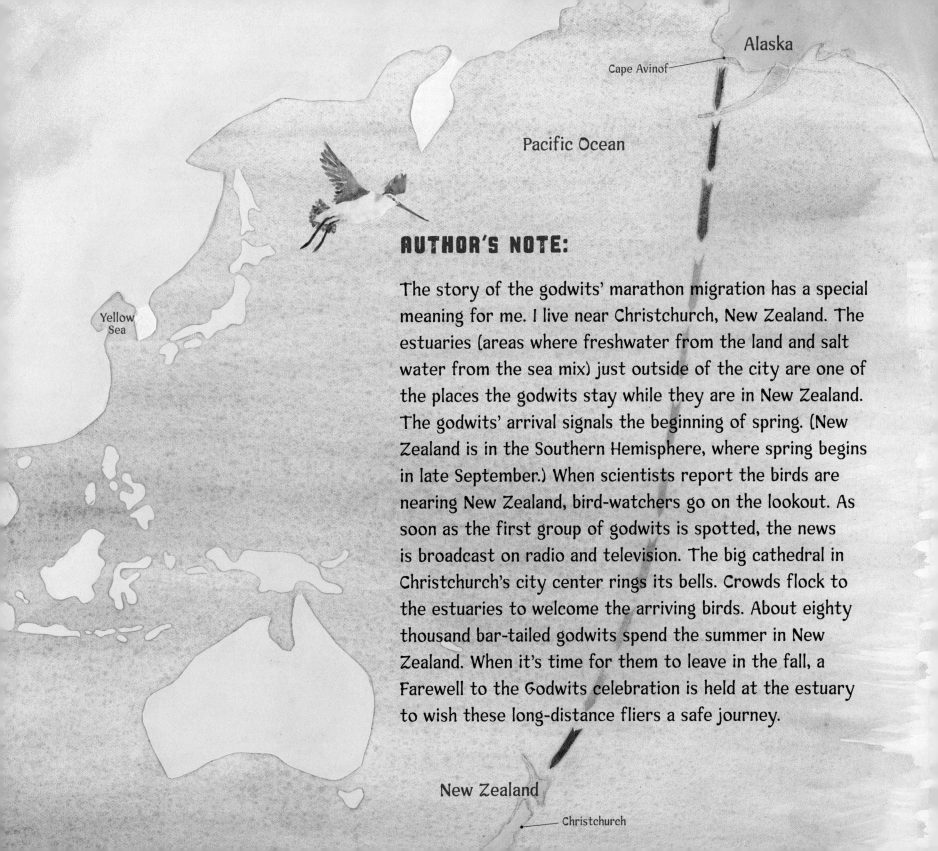

Alaska

Cape Avinof

Pacific Ocean

Yellow
Sea

AUTHOR'S NOTE:

The story of the godwits' marathon migration has a special meaning for me. I live near Christchurch, New Zealand. The estuaries (areas where freshwater from the land and salt water from the sea mix) just outside of the city are one of the places the godwits stay while they are in New Zealand. The godwits' arrival signals the beginning of spring. (New Zealand is in the Southern Hemisphere, where spring begins in late September.) When scientists report the birds are nearing New Zealand, bird-watchers go on the lookout. As soon as the first group of godwits is spotted, the news is broadcast on radio and television. The big cathedral in Christchurch's city center rings its bells. Crowds flock to the estuaries to welcome the arriving birds. About eighty thousand bar-tailed godwits spend the summer in New Zealand. When it's time for them to leave in the fall, a Farewell to the Godwits celebration is held at the estuary to wish these long-distance fliers a safe journey.

New Zealand

Christchurch